Dedicated to my family

John C. Curtis
"Dad"
Jennie Mae Cox Curtis
"Mama"

and my sisters	and my brothers
Hazel Mae Curtis	John Raymond Curtis
"Hazel"	"Ray"
Rose Marie Curtis	Walter David Curtis
"Marie"	"Walter"

"Miss Prim"
Jean Marian Curtis Hovenden
Author and Illustrator

Synopsis of My Childhood

I vividly remember the large, 200-acre farm where I lived during the years between 1920 and 1928. It seemed everything there had a special meaning to me . . . the big, white house surrounded by trees, a box elder tree in one corner of the yard. Our treehouse perched among its huge branches. The sidewalk from the backdoor passed the south side of the house, turned at the corner and continued on, meeting another one from the west porch and on to the front yard gate. In the semicircle by the gate stood one of four large catalpa trees in a row, spreading their shade over the yard and house. Soft maples and two tall spruce trees grew to the north of the yard. And, a big cherry tree stood directly in the east fence line. The flower and vegetable gardens were adjacent to the yard's south fence line.

The usual farm buildings were in the barnyard (west of the house yard). There was a chicken house and chicken yard south of the barnyard, followed by a long, red shed which housed a shop, machine shed and a storage section that held my folks' big surrey with little lamps. My brother and I played in the surrey and thought it special. Next, came the garage where Dad kept his Ford car. Two large grain bins were on either side of it . . . all under one long roof. Further to the west of the red shed, a hog house with upper windows stood. This was the farrowing house for the farm hogs. Beyond that, was a large double corn crib with a big corn dump, powered by one horse. It carried wagon loads of corn to the top of the crib roof, filling the two corncribs. To the west, was a red straw shed with stanchions for cows and a huge straw area, usually filled with oat straw at threshing time. In the west-center of the barnyard stood the big barn. A large horse head was painted on its north gable, the date, 1921, printed beneath it. It held stalls for eight head of horses and stanchions for eight head of cattle. A runway went through the center with two graineries on one side. A six foot square section held a ladder reaching up to the enormous haymow. On top of the cone on the barn's roof was a gold-colored horse weather vane.

North of the barn was a concrete watering tank, with a pipe in the center. Water bubbled up from it by means of the tall windmill, which stood over a ten-foot diameter cistern of water. The big wheel, with its fan, turned in the direction of the wind and pumped the tank full. It could be turned off by pulling down a wooden lever. A metal ladder on one corner rose to the top of the windmill. A big farm gate separated the barnyard from the road to the northeast.

Northeast of the house yard was a fifteen acre pasture where the horses stayed at night. To the south, a twenty acre pasture for cattle, corn fields, oatfields, and meadow made up our big farm.

This was the area I spent over eight years of my childhood. I described this farm and my childhood years there to my own children, many years later. They enjoyed hearing of my life there, living in this large, green-shuttered farm house. The following essays originated here between the years of 1920 and 1928.

The Sack Swing

My mother gave us rags and old materials to fill a gunny sack for a sack swing.

Far across to the end of the fifteen acre pasture was a huge, old willow with large limbs. My brother, Ray, Walter and I went to the old willow tree. Ray tied the rope on the sack and secured the other end to the big willow branch that spread out from the tree. We took turns running and jumping on the sack swing. It swept across the rippling grasses. It was like flying through the air . . . it looked like the swing swept out further than our tire swing in the yard. When it was still, it wasn't too high off the ground, and quite safe.

If I Could Go Back

Oh wouldn't you like to go back again,
To the summers of long ago.
Where the windy hills and lovely plains:
Beckon you to come and know
The peace of childhood years.
When life was rich and full:
If I could go back again
And be a child once more.

I'd take more time to realize:
How swiftly flies the May.
I'd take more note of clear June skies.
And meadows sweet with hay.
I'd live and laugh all summer long,
Not wish for a grown-up to be
Keeping in my heart a song
Of childhoods transiency.

The Orchard Where My Brother and I Played

It seemed larger, but was probably a 5 acre orchard with tall walnut trees to the south that we could climb . . . going out to the ends of branches, we would drop from the ends (probably no more than four feet) but, it seemed like quite a feat for us. There were numerous kinds of apple trees . . . we knew the ones that ripened quickest. Also, there was a tree with large, green and white flecked apples which remained very hard all fall long. Our Dad called these winter apples.

We made play houses of just flat boards outlining a square "room" on the green grass. We had an old boiler, bent in the center, a couch for our parlor. A tall metal drum-like can was our piano and a scratch with a finger nail across its surface brought goosebumps to our arms. This would happen by accident . . . never intentionally! We had a stump that served as a chair, since it had a higher piece on one side. Then, there were our small 1916 Ford tires which were red, gray and black. We ran along back of them, pushing them around the orchard . . . these were our dogs. Neatly, we would line them up in the playhouse.

We had friends, make-believe ones. I did most of the talking for them . . . a tall girl called Jennie Mare, a stupid boy named Blubber Mule. Another girl . . . Juicy Juice (named for a gum we had . . . Juicy Fruit).

We had the run of the two large pastures, one was 15-acres adjacent to the orchard, where we played with two wheels and a rod connecting them . . . probably back buggy wheels. The two of us ran side by side all over this short cropped grass pasture. Out in the center, we found yellow sorrel, tiny bell-shaped flowers of yellow. It was edible and my mother made us a tiny sorrel pie . . . it was fair tasting. My brother and I sat on the center of the connecting rod to the wheels and said we were at a show while we watched the sunset's rays filtering through a huge hedge west of the farm. We used these same two wheels for a merry-go-round, turning it with one wheel on the ground and the other over our heads. One would climb atop the wheel and the other stand on the bottom wheel (so it wouldn't upset). Then, slowly the one on the bottom would turn the top wheel, the top person feeling he was riding a merry-go-round.

One lovely day in summer, Walter and I longed for those reddest of cherries . . . the ones in the top of the big, cherry tree in the yard. We set about climbing it. It was nearing supper time, but we did climb it and the higher we climbed the redder the luscious cherries became. We were picking and eating among the red cherries and green leaves when, CRACK! And, we both settled down ten feet below. The big, cherry tree limb protected us as it touched the ground. There we sat on the broken limb, unharmed but terribly scared. We climbed through the leafy branches and ran for the back porch. We knew we shouldn't have climbed the tree. Walter was the bold one and called for Mama. But, it was Dad who came. He looked with disbelief at the big downed cherry tree limb and then at us. "Are you hurt?" We replied, "No" and he gathered us in his arms and was so glad we were safe. He explained how we could have broken arms or legs and pain. We listened and never again did we climb a cherry tree.

Barefoot Days

It was late May. The weather was warm and beautiful and green grass filled the yard. It was nearing time to "Go Barefoot." The thought of bare feet in the cool, green grass was exciting to my brother, Walter and me. No shoes to tie and if it rained, there would be puddles to run through and splash with our bare feet . . . especially the puddles by the rainspout off the house. To go barefoot meant it was summertime, but, it also meant an every night inspection of bare feet . . . feet that had to be scrubbed (not just washed), stains and scratches checked and many times an injury from a nail or sharp object that had been stepped on was treated. Dad usually treated such wounds with peroxide. One drop on the injury and it would foam up and then be covered with a bandage.

To prevent nail or glass wounds, Walter and I were each issued a half gallon pail. We would go all over the yard and orchard, picking up every nail, piece of glass and metal that could injure a running foot. This took several days, and our dad would tell us when he thought we had it clear of debris. Shortly, that day came. Oh, we were so happy! We walked carefully at first, and then, as our feet toughened, we could even run near the ash pile and it wouldn't hurt. However, even with our precautions, there were still times when we accidentally stepped on a nail in a board and had to have it cleaned and treated. Then, we would walk, favoring the injured area until it healed. We seldom had any bad injuries.

To make sure we scrubbed the roughened skin on our soles well each night, we were promised a box of Cracker Jack . . . with a surprise in it. Every Saturday night, Mama or Dad would slip a box of Cracker Jack under our pillows. I could hear Walter yelling on Sunday morning, with delight, from his bedroom. He had found a little, metal knife in his box. It wasn't too sharp, but could cut an apple. I found a whistle in mine. It was loud and I was happy with it. It was made of metal too. Walter and I liked the Sunday Comics and each Sunday, we had a page that had black and white comics. By using a paint brush and water, they would color up and look nice. There was Barney Google and his horse, Sparky. There was the Peter Rabbit family.

Summer neared its end and we had new shoes. Our "Barefoot Days" were over, but we had enjoyed a childhood's happy summer. It brought to mind Whittier's poem, "Barefoot Boy" . . .

"Every evening, from thy feet,
Shall the cool wind kiss the heat
All too soon, those feet must hide
In the prison cells of pride."

The Owl and Ray

On the old Bocock place were many trees. Walter and I knew the names of most of them. One particularly large tree at the entrance to the farmyard was a cottonwood and white cotton floated on the air every spring. It was about 500 feet from the house yard fence. Two tall spruce trees grew just inside the yard fence. One evening, our brother Ray, wearing his ball cap, stood in the center . . . between the pines and the cottonwood (or, "Old Stark Tree" as Walter and I called it). Ray was imitating the barn owls. An owl would swoop down toward Ray on its way to the cottonwood tree, clicking its bill. Ray was surprised, but continued to harass the owl by imitating its call perfectly. This time, the owl swooped down low enough to pick Ray's cap off his head and drop it close by him. That did it! Ray disappeared from the scene. The owl was too close for comfort. We all laughed at that.

Tragedy

Walter and I were saddened by the death of our cat, Midnight . . . a black kitten. One of a litter, but somehow he died. Maybe an old tom did it, but we never knew.

To add some dignity to his death, we decided to bury him with pomp and circumstance. We dug a square hole out under the last walnut tree to the west, lined it with grass and wrapped the kitten in a piece of cloth. We slowly covered it. It must have been 12 to 14 inches deep. We piled dirt to make a little mound . . . and then, forgot all about it.

Rains came and went and the grave was almost covered by leaves and weeds. One day, we thought about Midnight and what was happening to him. We decided to unearth him and see for ourselves if he was even there. We had sticks strong enough to raise the earth little by little. We couldn't find anything at first . . .

Then, the stick caught on a dark object. It looked oily. Shocked, we quickly recovered the whole place and heaped leaves and more dirt to make it a mound.

We seemed to grow in our reasoning of death . . . that it is so final. We never mentioned the episode again.

At Night Time

All is dark and still,
Save an echo from the hill;
And a robin's trill,
At night time.

A star studded sky,
And bats darting by;
Always on the fly,
At night time.

Loudly calls the whippoor-will;
From it's home by the rill;
Then again all is still,
At night time.

Memories of Childhood Years

About as far back as I can remember, I was sitting on my Mother's lap. We were riding in my Dad's car and he was driving. I don't remember if my brothers or sisters were with us. It was a hot summer day and I was thirsty. As the car neared the Spoon River, I saw rippling water flowing within its banks. My thirst increased and I stretched my arms forward, calling "River Please."

One afternoon, my brother Ray had misbehaved. My Dad said to him, "I'll comb your hair . . . and I won't use the comb!" I quickly said, "Then, you'll use the brush!"

Eggs

Near Easter, my brother, Walter and I had eggs in an old oil stove. We had a bucket of eggs safely placed there to bring in on Easter morning. Our brother, Ray had his rifle and was cleaning it at a distance from us. He held it up and said he would use the old oil stove as a target. Walter and I screamed and begged him not to. He was surprised at our reaction and went to the stove. Removing the door, he looked inside to find our collection of eggs and said we should have told him there were eggs in there. It was to be our Easter surprise and we wanted to keep it from him too. Luckily, he looked to see why we screamed.

Pasture Pigs

One day, Dad was talking to a salesman on the front porch. He was trying to sell hog troughs and other farm equipment. I sat on the porch listening to them and perked my ears up when I heard the man say, quote, "When your hogs dig up their little pigs . . ." Dad and he looked at each other and went down to the barn to finish discussing business away from little ears.

The next day, I saw a large hog crossing the middle part of the hog pasture. It circled around and wandered off toward the rest of the hogs. I walked out to where this hog had been, carefully watching the ground, hoping to find a dug~up area and possibly some little pigs. Didn't the man say, "When your hogs dig up their pigs?" . . . It was a fruitless task and I forgot about it until one day when my dad took me through the long hog house. There were lots of pens with doors connecting each one and a door to the walk way. In there, Dad walked, holding me up high, so I could see the mama hogs and their piglets, all black, with a white band around their shoulders. It was scary, as the big hogs would snort and sound mean when one of the babies squealed. Up high, toward the roof, was a row of small windows that let in the sunlight.

Walter didn't go through the hog house, as he was afraid and too small. This day, I learned pigs weren't really dug up out in the pasture.

The Yard Stick

Walter and I had a 36-inch yard stick . . . 1 inch at the top and 1/4 inch at the bottom. I would walk it around and talk for it. We named it "Kid." As we got used to playing and talking for it, we called it "Old Kid." We took it everywhere and tied a small, old shoe of ours on the bottom of the stick. We took it to the tree house and in our tire swing . . . and out to the orchard to meet the other imaginary people of ours . . . Like Jennie Mare, Juicy Juice and Blubber Mule.

We climbed a tree that had a limb over the old, outdoor toilet, taking Kid with us. We decided to look down the little, white chimney on its roof. Seeing cobwebs, we lowered Old Kid to clear out the webs, but in the process, I accidentally dropped Kid down the chimney.

I implored our Dad to get Kid out, but he was firm. Kid must stay there . . . and, so, alas for Kid.

Cloud Stairways to Cloud Homes

On warm summer afternoons, Walter and I played in the little 15 acre pasture northeast of our house. Walter decided the sky above the pasture was his home and that his name was Walter Anderson. We looked at the clouds that looked like stair steps . . . wide steps to the sky, and visioned beautiful rooms in the clouds.

I was not to be outdone, so I said the 20 acre pasture south and adjacent to the yard's garden and orchard was MY pasture and the sky above was my home. It too had cloud formations looking like a huge stairway of steps and I, too had lovely rooms, and that my name was Jean Alahanded!

We enjoyed these fantasies in those long-ago summertime days in memory.

Summer Tragedy

One day, I took my precious box outside. It held my treasures, including favorite books . . . "Annie and Willie's Prayer," "The Night Before Christmas" and "Peter Pan" (a much older and different story than the one most people think of). Our mother had read them to us many times. I liked the story of "Peter Pan" and loved the pictures inside . . . of his bird nest boat and his harp playing picture. We had tried to make a boat (Walter and I) but, couldn't find enough twigs and couldn't make those that we did hold together.

I even had my doll, a small painted face and painted hair girl, wrapped up in her blanket and carefully placed in the box with my books. I set it in my playhouse, a wood-edged square out in the orchard. I forgot to bring it back inside, as Mama said I must do, if I took it out. It was in the middle of the night when I thought of it again . . . my box . . .

The rain pelted on the kitchen's metal roof. Lightning flashed. Thunder roared! I was devastated . . . too frightened to even go look out the window, as flash after flash of lightning lit up the pouring rain. I felt so badly about my box, but then I finally slept and when I awakened, the bedroom was full of sunshine.

I quickly dressed and raced out to get my box. It had lost its shape. The doll was wet, but I could see her face colors yet. One hand was washed away. The doll was so dear to me, that even in her bad condition, I thought of the poem Mama had once told me . . . that a little girl's doll had been trodden on by the cows, yet the little girl said she was the prettiest doll in the world. That's how I felt too. Mama helped me with the wet books. We dried the book pages and we could still read the stories, but the leaves were torn loose and had to be held together.

It was a sad lesson. However, I did learn to keep my pretty things in the house. So ended a "Summer Tragedy."

The Meories and the Keeks

Walter and I played in the sunny orchard. It was mid-Summer, warm and humid. We sat in our swings and decided we would like to be a new animal . . . one that could yell . . . and run . . . and climb. And, pick strawberries as their food. We crawled along the south garden fence into the pasture lot path. Our hands were our gathering devices and our stomachs were our baskets. We told our mother we had turned into Meories, but were a tame animal . . . She gave us each a big sorghum cookie and told us to go play in the yard. We had a wagon and loaded it with long cut grasses from the yard's mowing. After making a little haystack, we were tired and went back into the house for something cold to drink.

A week or so later, we were tired of the tame Meory animal and wanted to be a wild animal . . . one that yelled "Keek-Keek-Keek, So It Is." We ran and played out in the little fifteen acre pasture and hid in trees and bushes. We were the Wild Keeks! We broke off pieces from the base of the boxelder trees. These bushy growths with the pretty green leaves we tied to our backs. The leafy top shielded our heads from the sun.

After a few days, we tired of "The Wild Keeks" and again played in our yard with our toys.

The Sorghum Jug

Summer or winter, we had buckwheat pancakes for breakfast at our house. Nearly every morning, we all enjoyed them with our sausage cakes. Mama would use a small, stone jar to mix up the batter, carefully saving out about a cup of the "rising batter" for the next day's pancakes "start." The buckwheat flour was gray in color and had a delicious flavor! We poured brown molasses called sorghum slowly over the cakes. It was heavy and dark colored, so we would add some butter and stir well. A creamy, tan molasses resulted . . . how good it was! Later on, Dad brought home a half gallon of a new syrup called Confection Syrup. It was great . . . Light and honey colored, and for a while, it took over the sorghum-molasses spotlight. Still, we used sorghum as a syrup for our buckwheat cakes and Mama made big sorghum cookies and gingerbread with it. Dad bought it by the gallon from my Swedish Uncle Charlie who grew the cane in his fields and then, boiled down its juices to a certain stage of thickness.

We used sorghum to make taffy, but not too often, as it always became a sticky affair. Mama cooked the taffy and when it was time to pull, we all buttered our clean hands to prevent sticking. As we children stretched and pulled the pliable masses, they became a very light tan. We were having a great time, pulling and eating, until a chunk became stuck in Walter's curly hair. It took a while for Mama to get him cleaned up. I longed to have his yellow curls . . . my hair was so straight and plain light brown. Once, I asked my mother why I couldn't have the curls in the family? After all, I reasoned, girls needed curly hair. It was wasted on boys. She consoled me, saying I had perfect, straight roots. However, that night, she braided my hair and the next morning when she let it out, I was delighted with the pretty curls . . . that is, until the curls had to be combed and became not-so-pretty snarls. My older sister, Hazel patiently combed them free, strand by strand. When I would complain how the snarls hurt, she would play a game. "These snarls want to stay in your hair and when I get them out, they put their handkerchiefs over their heads and cry." Of course, I knew it was far-fetched, but it helped to think about it that way, and so, I was able to stand a lot more "snarl-pulling pain." At the age of six, my sister, Hazel drove me to Bradford, Illinois, six miles north of our place to get my hair "bobbed." It was cut short and I had bangs. I felt so happy and free as we bounced home in the buggy. It was rarely used as we had a car, but since roads could be a problem when mud hit the axles we were happy to have it and also the spring-seated wagon, known as The Democrat. The Democrat would get Dad to town for groceries in Wyoming (Illinois) during rainy weather and in winter when nothing else could.

Many years later, I bought a sorghum jug from the family of that same uncle who had made sorghum back when I was a small child. Now, I look at it, with its unique glaze . . . a brown glob of special lacquer here and there, resembling spilling-over sorghum. It is probably a five gallon container, with a glistening glaze. I keep it in my kitchen year-round now, with artificial flowers arranged in it to suit the season. In springtime, pink and white dogwood graces its mouth. In summer, assorted colors of zinnias, autumn—maple leaves and brown cat tails and winter—red poinsettias nestle in green fern fronds. All make a lovely decoration and the jug brings to mind days when sorghum was an everyday staple in my mother's kitchen.

Maple Syrup Time

I like maple syrup time,
When the maple trees we tap:
Hanging pails to each one,
To catch the dripping sap.

When the sap is in the vat,
We start the old wood fire:
And keep it filled with boiling sap,
Boiling, long after we retire.

Within a day or so,
It has boiled down just fine:
To fill the jars in a row,
At maple syrup time.

At the Ice Cream Parlor

One summer afternoon, my Dad had an occasion to go to Camp Grove and he asked me if I'd like to ride along. I was elated. My mother combed my hair and tied a blue ribbon to hold it back. She let me wear my white dress and long white stockings and shoes. I walked in style, I thought, holding my Dad's hand. We entered Camp Grove's only ice cream parlor where the little table at which we sat had a round white top and wire-like legs that curved nicely to form the base of the table. The chair I sat on was a wire clad one, a circle back and seat and curved wire legs. It was elegant and I ate my ice cream carefully so as not to spill any on my white dress. The man who brought our ice cream was most polite.

I was so thrilled Dad had treated me to ice cream on that long-ago summer afternoon.

Ice Cream On the 4th of July

Fourth of July was special at our house. In the afternoon, our dad would bring a container of vanilla ice cream, a white cardboard box with a bright gold wire handle. As he brought it in, Mama would unpack it quickly to prevent the melting of our delicious ice cream.

Our mother had the yellow and white checked table cloth spread on the table with the children in their places . . . spoons in hand. Each received a nice dish full of the cream-colored dessert. It seemed nothing could ever taste so delicious. That was our special treat for the Fourth of July.

One July 4th, we were all gathered together at the Wyoming fairgrounds, sitting in the bleachers, awaiting the lighting of a huge firecracker. It was out in the center of the arena. It looked like a red barrel, tall and round, and to be exploded. Fear and excitement abounded among the crowd. When the lighted wick neared the end, we held our breath . . . then, a huge bang and the whole firecracker ripped open and out jumped a colorful clown. Oh, we thought it exciting!

My best memory of that celebration was of the two colorful balloons I had and a Kewpie Doll my aunt gave me . . . a gorgeous painted and colorful doll of plaster of Paris. It was very breakable. As I was getting out of the car, it fell and its head broke off. But, both head and body were intact, so my mother wrapped a medium size corncob and stuck it in the Kewpie's neck cavity. Then, she secured the head back on and it looked perfect. With its features and bright feathers, I thought it the most glamorous doll I'd ever owned.

"The Old Covered Bridge"

The old covered bridge looks
a little lorn,
A few boards loose - it's
shingles torn.
But over the river,
its ancient span,
Still serves as a crossing
for beast and man.
Beneath it, water flows
dark and deep.
Where boulders are mossy,
the shore is steep.
Above it, the suns of many
seasons ago,
Have weathered its shingles
and timbers below.
Serving all who pass its way,
a noble structure, it stands today.

The Telephone

The telephone was the communication line for people . . . especially in the country. It was a respected object, hung on the wall that announced calls in either short or long rings. Our ring was three shorts.

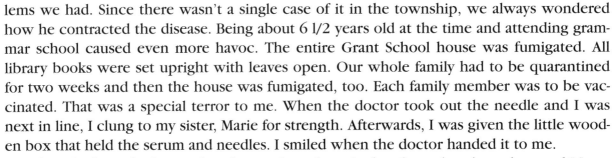

One morning, the phone rang its three shorts and Dad answered. It was a big "Hello." The person calling asked him if he had Prince Albert in a can . . . that was a prominent tobacco name. Dad hesitated, but was a smoker of that brand, so answered, "Yes, I have." The caller shouted, "Well, let him out!", laughed and hung up the phone. Later on, Mama answered our short rings to hear a lady's voice asking, "Are you the lady that washes?" Indignantly, she retorted, "No! Of course not!" "Why you dirty thing!" quipped the caller and hung up . . . homespun jest. But, my folks guessed who it was and laughed too.

The telephone was helpful in times of emergency and we always had one. Our doctor lived eight miles away over muddy roads. Paved roads had not come to our area yet. My brother Walter's scarlet fever disease was one of the worst problems we had. Since there wasn't a single case of it in the township, we always wondered how he contracted the disease. Being about 6 1/2 years old at the time and attending grammar school caused even more havoc. The entire Grant School house was fumigated. All library books were set upright with leaves open. Our whole family had to be quarantined for two weeks and then the house was fumigated, too. Each family member was to be vaccinated. That was a special terror to me. When the doctor took out the needle and I was next in line, I clung to my sister, Marie for strength. Afterwards, I was given the little wooden box that held the serum and needles. I smiled when the doctor handed it to me.

The telephone had a speaker that projected ten inches from the phone box and Mama would tilt it upward during electrical storms. This was because, during a bad storm, at one time, fire had shot from the speaker at a close strike of lightning. It was feared . . . and loved . . .

Invitations would come over the phone. When neighbors held what they called a "Shin-Dig"it meant that the rugs would be rolled back and a party with square dancing or slow waltzes was coming. The violinist was Chief, our neighbor and my dad would play the banjo and mouth harp. The piano player would be a neighbor lady. The "Caller" was Chief's grandson or my dad, who was a good Caller also. "Dosie-Do and chicken in a bread pan kickin' out dough" puzzled me. But, the dancers knew what it meant and "Promenade All" sent them into a circle with crossed hands. It was all a part of square dancing. I only attended one of these house parties at a close neighbor's and enjoyed the refreshments served at the late hour of ten o'clock. The parties never lasted long, as children grew tired and they were family-type gatherings.

The telephone brought an invitation to go to Aunt Minnie's for Sunday dinner. At once, visions of roast beef and Aunt Minnie's mashed potatoes appeared. She could beat potatoes into mounds of fluffy whiteness and her iced layer cake was the best. There was a beautiful, square glass honey dish with matching lid, full of honey in the comb. I almost always choked on the extreme sweetness . . . and too large a portion. But, with a glass of Aunt Minnie's cold well water, I always recovered to eat the rest of that wonderful meal. Aunt Minnie was known for her excellent cooking ability.

Then, the telephone brought messages of sadness . . . deaths of out-of-state relatives . . . or in the immediate neighborhood. And Dad's serious look as he put up the receiver and started for the door, going to offer his personal help to any bereaved family in the area. He was almost always the first to offer help in any way he could. I remember that so vividly and respected him even more.

The telephones were a very important part of a family's life, and kept people in close contact when there were no pavements and roads were sometimes impassable. And, when not used for emergencies, they were a grapevine connection for the neighborhood gossip and entertainment too, for anybody could listen in on anyone else's call.

"Little Path"

I followed a narrow winding path
In the early spring,

I saw the violets shyly peep
From beneath their leaves of green.

The path wound 'round a little bend
And crossed a meadow wide,

To where a rippling stream flowed
On the other side.

It crossed the stream from stone
To stone and led on up the hill,

And there was lost among the trees
Where all was green and still.

I saw the valley down below
Bathed in sunset's light,

Saw the wild birds swiftly fly
On their homeward flight.

The little path had led me there,
Where springtime beauty was everywhere.

Going to Aunt Minnie's

Going to visit our Aunt Minnie was a joy that we looked forward to. Our mother had called Aunt Minnie and she was expecting us for a noon dinner. So, on that sunny June morning, we were all ready when our dad brought the Model T Ford to the front gate. The weather had to be dry. or we would not have been able to drive through the Spoon River bottom land. And, Aunt Minnie's home was on the other side.

As we neared her home, I could see her gabled, cream-colored house. We turned the corner and there it was, in a big yard circled by a white picket fence and many tall sugar maple trees. These shaded the porches that encircled three sides of the house. The concrete sidewalks girdled the house, also, and led to three driveways. I knew my cousins would pull the red wagon, with me in it, on those sidewalks.

We were met at the door by Aunt Minnie with her "Well, for pity's sake, do come in," and she hugged and kissed us and led us into her pretty living room. Soon, the table was filled with delicious food . . . tender roast beef piled on a huge platter, a mound of whipped potatoes in a white, ironstone bowl, freshly made cottage cheese. The cut glass, lidded honey dish was close by me. The golden, amber honey in the square comb tasted delicious with Aunt Minnie's snowflake rolls and freshly churned butter. She poured amber coffee for the adults and cold milk for the rest of us. Aunt Minnie's dessert was a big, white coconut layer cake with fluffy, white icing. A large bowl of crushed and sugared strawberries was passed and we ate them with yellow cream. The meal was eaten with the happy voices of the family, mingled with laughter and compliments on Aunt Minnie's wonderful meal.

The afternoon was spent visiting. I went into Aunt Minnie's beautiful parlor where an ornate stand stood in the center of the room with a heavy, lace spread over it. On top of the stand were two picture albums with large covers of crushed plush . . . one in red and the other of golden plush. Above the stand, the chandelier lights hung with five lamps and glass chimneys. Each lamp was surrounded by five cut glass prisms, hanging. Aunt Minnie lowered the chandelier with a chain and lighted the lamps at my request, then raised it high and the light flickered over the whole room. These were carbide lamps. The big, tall square Victrola and pump organ gleamed in the light. On, through the tasseled drapes was a small room near the front of the house. There sat a mahogany loveseat and two matching chairs. The loveseat had a soft, green velvet covering. And, sitting on it were The Three Bears, with orange-brown fur. Mama, Papa and Baby Bear. I was allowed to hold them for awhile. As I sat on the loveseat, I looked west to the front door. The faint pink of the coming late afternoon sky filtered through the frosted glass in the top center of the outside door. It was a frosty scene of deer in a woods . . . I thought it was so pretty. Aunt Minnie had fancy chocolate boxes with beautiful colored ribbons and bows. She gave the boxes to my brother, Walter and the ribbons and bows to me. I was so happy with these satin beauties. I could wear them in my light brown, shoulder length hair.

After awhile, we went out to sit in their large yard. I tried the hammock tied between two trees, but kept falling out. My brother was smaller, so he could stay in it better. I walked over to the large circle of clam shells. They were all wired together to form a solid three foot wide and four foot high clam shell pile. My uncle had made it from the many clam shells from the Indian Creek and Spoon River at that time. The river ran through the bottom land of his big farm and Indian Creek ran adjacent to the west boundary, so he had plenty of them to make this pile. My cousin had pulled Walter and me in his red wagon all around the sidewalks and we thought it great fun. The day was ending and as we were about to leave, Aunt Minnie gave my mother a large bouquet of her fragrant cabbage roses. She also gave us several quarts of ripe strawberries from their large patch. It had been a wonderful day for all of us.

Clam shell pile at Aunt Minnies

Mrs. McCuen's Little Girl for a Day

On a bright, June morning, the telephone rang. It was our nearest neighbor to the west of us—Mrs. McCuen. She told Mama, her daughter (who was my sister Hazel's best friend) was visiting relatives in Minnesota and she wondered if I could come down and visit her for the day. Of course, Mama said "Yes," and that I would walk down and for her to call back when I arrived.

I wore a blue dress and my hair was brushed. I was so excited . . . the idea of a whole day's visit at a home where there still sat three teddy bears on a couch that belonged to a grown-up girl and had been left as a decoration . . . three honey colored bears!

I tripped lightly the nearly mile distance to their house. Mrs. McCuen was waiting at her gate. I was a little afraid of the dog at first. But, he wagged his tail, so I knew he was friendly. She took me into the house and showed me little novelties she had saved from her "Mother's Oats" cereal boxes. Each box had held a gift . . . a salt and pepper shaker set, a cereal bowl and a vinegar cruet. She put them in a box for me to take home. I was so happy. Mrs. McCuen told me we were having fried chicken for dinner and that we should go pick some strawberries for a fresh strawberry shortcake and cream for dinner. I took the quart box and she a large pan and out we went, into the sunlit strawberry patch. She let me wear her daughter's straw hat to keep from getting sunburned. I looked around . . . green fields on every side, farm houses here and there and I saw Mr. McCuen and their son plowing corn. Wild roses grew to the east edge of the strawberry patch. Oh, the strawberries were so large! And, smelled so good! After I had about half a box picked, I ate several of the largest ones and then continued to fill the box heaping full . . . with extra large ones on the top. We stemmed berries on her porch where wild grapevines shaded the whole south side. It was so pleasant. We talked of threshing time to come in July and what stories I liked best. She said her daughter would be home that weekend from visiting cousins in Minnesota.

I could smell the chicken frying and she had mashed potatoes and gravy, fresh green snap beans, radishes, green onions and lettuce from her big garden. I helped set the table and was glad Mama had taught me how to place the fork on one side and knife and spoon on the other. The tablecloth had strawberry designs at the corners. I carefully put a napkin at each place. She made lemonade and served it in goblets . . . oh, it was such a pretty table. At noon, everything was ready and in came Mr. McCuen and their son, who said, "I thought I saw two people in the strawberry patch." And, Mrs. McCuen replied, "Yes, I had Jean come to visit me and be my little girl for a day." I was so pleased and smiled my appreciation.

We had our dinner and I felt at home . . . not the least bit shy. I was taking her daughter's place for a day and felt so proud. After the last of the shortcake and lemonade, we sat awhile and visited. Then, the men went outside and I helped clear the table and wiped dishes . . . carefully, so as not to break one. Mrs. McCuen finished up the dishes, then, picking up the braided rug by the range, she took the teakettle of boiling water and poured it all over the already clean, wooden floor. Then, she mopped and wiped until it shone. Oh, it looked so fresh and neat.

I held the teddy bears. They were old and delicate, so I had to be careful while holding them. Afterwards, we went out to gather eggs, as the day was warm and she wanted to put them in the cool basement, in the egg case. It was a big, square wooden box with slots and held twelve dozen eggs. She would sell them at the grocery store on Saturdays. I held a fuzzy, yellow baby duck. I thought it cuter than a baby chick. We looked at her flowers and roses . . . they were all in bloom. She picked a bouquet of red and pink roses, wrapped them in a wet cloth and put them in a sack with a quart of strawberries and my trinkets from the oat boxes. At 3:30, she called my mother and told her I was on my way home. She seemed pleased with me and kissed me goodbye and said I should come again for a day. I said I would and thanked her. Soon, I was on my way home, full of excitement to tell everyone about my happy day. When I got home, Mama called Mrs. McCuen, while I showed my cereal dish with blue rim and a red flower in the center, the glass salt and pepper shaker set and the glass vinegar cruet. Mama appreciated the strawberries and we set the vase of roses in the center of the dining table.

I had had a day I would always remember. A week later, two other ladies asked Mama if I could visit them for a day, but I never did get to go. Mrs. Davidson's house was like a mansion, with two stairways and a big summer kitchen that looked like a little house. But, I only saw it from the outside and loved the long, sweeping lawn with two rows of tall spruce trees. It wasn't so I could visit these two ladies, but, I was Mrs. McCuen's Little Girl For A Day!

Threshing Time

At Geary's, the big threshing machine was still running and the stars were almost visible. We could hear the engine from our house, and then it stopped, and the job at Geary's was finished at last. The men on hay racks hurried home, glad to be finished with another farm. Next, was our place in the threshing run. The big, black machine came huffing and puffing down the road toward our barn yard gate. We watched from the yard as it neared the driveway, belching dark smoke. And, then, slowly it turned in, being careful the big separator didn't bump the gate.

On it puffed, till it was in the twenty acre pasture south of our house. There it set while the machine men prepared it for the night. They always stayed with their machine as was the custom, throughout the threshing run. Walter and I were so excited and happy that tomorrow was Threshing Day At Our House!

Our dad had already borrowed a table and chairs from Mahler's (one of our neighbors) to add to our two tables. A long table was created and it reached through the big dining room, for all the threshing crew were to eat dinner and possibly supper at our house. Lots of preparations were made . . . Mama had been working toward this for weeks. She had made pickled beets from our garden and the cabbage and onions for making coleslaw were home grown, too. Neighbor ladies had promised to help out and Mama had hired a lady to help who had a reputation for knowing everything about feeding twenty or more men at a Threshing Dinner, and on time, too. As it turned out, she caused Mama some regret and astonishment when she took almost a whole remaining raisin pie and threw it into the chicken yard. Raisins rolled on the ground and chickens dashed after them. Usually, raisin pies kept well (for at least two days) in the cool pie cupboard. To my mother, this seemed a bit on the wasteful side as she later confided to my dad. The next year, another lady took her place. But, back to the story . . .

Dad had gone early next morning to the Camp Grove store for a huge beef roast, wieners and a wheel of cheese and "boughten bread" as I called it, to go along with Mama's dinner rolls. The ladies came and two girl friends of my older sisters, Hazel and Marie had agreed to help wait on the tables. The meal was progressing fine by 10:30. . . beef roasting, chicken frying, pies baking. The cakes were baked the day before. The potatoes were pared, the cabbage was shredded and the big table was set. One neighbor brought her water cooler. It stood on legs and was full of ice for cooling drinking water and water for making lemonade. She was standing by it, I remember, when she put her hand on my head and said, "You are a nice little girlie." I felt proud. I was too young to pour water or lemonade at the table while the men were eating. My older sisters and their girl friends had that job and did it with such grace. I thought I might never be able to do that.

By noon, Mama had the white linen towels with the fine red line on each side all hung up by the big boxelder tree in the corner of the yard . . . the one with our treehouse high overhead. The water buckets were full and several wash pans were on a bench with bars of soap beside them. The whistle blew on the threshing machine and the dusty, tired men lined up at the washing area. Then, in they came to that monumental dinner. I believe there were fourteen places at the table that year.

After they had all eaten, and the last of the men had finished their dessert of pie, cake, lemonade and coffee, they all filed out. Before long, the whistle blew and all the men returned to the fields and their work of bringing in load after load of oat bundles for the big machine. Now it was time to clear the table and reset it for the meal for the women and children. I enjoyed the mashed potatoes and gravy, meats and peas. The raisin pie was my choice for dessert. It was so nice to eat and listen to the ladies talking.

Outside, I watched the big straw stack grow taller and wider as the straw flew out of the machine. It seemed so huge. I remembered how our dad had warned us we could not go near it for months . . . until rains and many of them had settled the straw. Then, we could climb to the top and slide down over the big sides of the stack. But, Dad would let us know when that would be. We knew the danger of sinking under the straw and soon dying . . .

But, for now, it was nice to watch its formation and all the excitement, people, food and we children slept soundly that night.

After the Threshing Was Over

After the big event of the summer time . . . Threshing Time was over, Walter and I played with the mown yard grass Dad had finished mowing. We piled it high in our wagon and hauled it to the orchard, placing it under two apple trees which grew close together. There, we made our OWN little haystack. It dried and grew small, but had that lovely smell of mown hay and we loved it.

One day, we decided we should move our playhouse to the far end of the little 15 acre cornfield southeast of our orchard. We carried some of our boards to form a room. We carried it to the south end of the cornfield, keeping in the row and going straight. At a large hedge row at the south end, we laid our board down, both getting stuck by hedge thorns. But, we continued. I carried the old boiler and Walter rolled the big, round can we called the piano. When we were half way across, we grew so tired, sweaty and hungry, we decided to leave the stump-chair and can piano in the field. We came back to the house to eat and rest. Dad, having already seen the stump and can said it was our job to bring it all back to the orchard . . . and we did, but, not with the gusto that we started out to move the playhouse.

My Mother's "Wild Greens"

It was a warm, sunny morning in mid-May. Mama had been out to the garden all morning and by ten thirty, she came into the house pulling off her Panama straw hat. "Whew, whew ! It's so hot in the garden! " In her hands, she was carrying a large milk pail full of greens. They were fresh-picked and "looked", . . . ready to be washed and cooked for our dinner. I loved greens and so I helped Mama wash them in cold water at the well. She let me help wash them and explained the virtues of the lowly dandelion. She showed the buds in its center. That was more proof that it was a dandelion. According to Mama, the dandelion got its name from its leaves. They are jagged and resemble the teeth of a lion. Its blooms are a bright yellow and children love to pick them for a golden bouquet. Sometimes, holding a dandelion flower under your chin would produce a golden glow. This meant you "liked butter." It is a weed and the flowers can be used in making dandelion wine or for medicine.

Mama's greens included some wild lettuce. It has to be very young or it will taste bitter. She had sourdock. Its tapering leaves were easy to wash. The majority of her pail contained the leaves of fresh, tender lambs quarter. It tastes like fresh, green spinach. She couldn't find any pepper grass, so she cut tender leaves from the horseradish plants for that added special taste to her wild greens. As she washed them, she'd tell me how to identify them, so in after years I could pick greens with safety, as she did. Mama put the cleaned greens in a large kettle with water, pieces of bacon, several potatoes and cooked them on the wood stove. When served, it was a meal in itself. Dad always sprinkled vinegar on his greens, but I liked mine as they came from the kettle, with the green colored potatoes and for dessert . . . fresh baked corn bread and sorghum and milk and coffee to drink. It was a May Time Dinner at Noon to remember.

"Mother"

Often I think of her dear face,
No other one can take her place;
My Mother,

Singing to sleep each child with bliss,
Curing each hurt with a mother's kiss;
My Mother,

Teaching the way of truth and life,
Shielding her baby's from every strife,
My Mother

Depriving herself yet always glad,
Hoping for them, joys she's never had;
My Mother

And as she receives each childish kiss,
It pays for the pleasures that she has missed,
My Mother

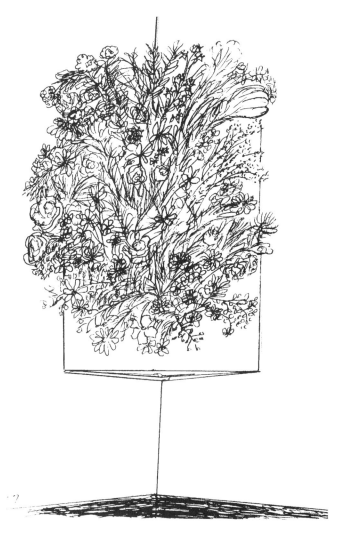

Corner Bouquet

In the northeast corner of the living room was a special thing of beauty that my mother worked on throughout the year. It started with a large brown metal flower holder with a frame covered in golden colored designs. In the center, was an oval hole, exposing a wide cavity in which dried flowers were placed. My mother's flower garden had bright red cockscomb flowers. When picked and dried, they would hold their color. She used cockscomb for the base of her bouquet and intermingled dried straw flowers . . . also from her garden. Mama enjoyed arranging and rearranging them, adding baby's breath and many wild plants and grasses. She had dark brown dried sourdock seed clusters, several sprays of dried pepper grass with its tiny seed pods. There was the yellow nut grass that grew in the damp areas of the orchard. This plant is really a sedge, not a grass. It has brown, fan-shaped flowers that are pretty when dried. She had yellow foxtail grasses. Its dried seed head looks like a fox's tail and blended well with the rest of the dried flowers.

Mama made these dried flowers look like a living flower bouquet and the whole family enjoyed them and learned to identify plants, especially wild plants and their seeds. Most of them grew on the farm where we lived.

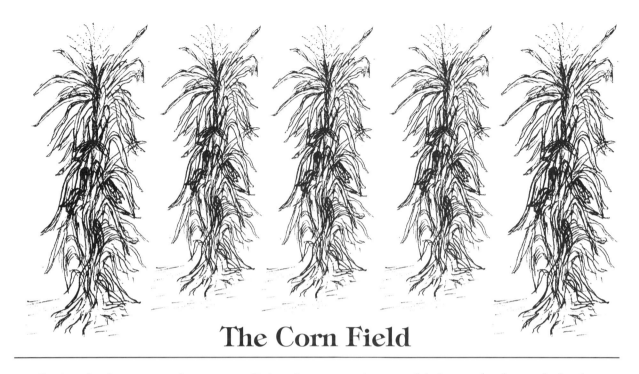

The Corn Field

Spring had come and we were living in a greening world. I watched my dad rake up cornstalks into long rows in the fifteen acre cornfield southeast of the orchard. The field cornered next to the orchard and I could watch the rake gathering up cornstalks from last year's harvest. All the ears had been picked last fall and now, the raking took place. At night, Dad would set fire to the long windrows of raked up stalks. It was a fascinating sight . . . we children sat on a blanket and watched the fire leap along the rows, sending sparks into the darkness. Frogs sang from the pond in the big twenty acre pasture to the west. This was the first process in preparation of the land for spring planting. Disking, plowing, and harrowing, then cross harrowing would make the field smooth as a garden. Dad had a special team of horses he used to pull the corn planter at the proper speed to plant. I could hear the click, click of the planter the next day. Every click meant seeds were going into the ground. When it was all planted, the long track of the planter ran through the field, showing where the hills of corn were. Rains came and warm weather. Before long, small, green plants dotted the entire field.

One moist, hot night in July, my Dad said, "That field of corn will rise two to three inches tonight." It grew tall, with tapering leaves and yellow tassels tossing in the wind. By September, Dad would cut cornstalks and throw them over the fence to feed the hogs and cattle in the pasture. He cut two stalks of corn and made two corn fiddles for Walter and me. First, he cut two slits on each stalk and raised up the strip and fastened with two small pieces of corn stalk at each end. Two pieces of a corn stalk make a fiddle, one is the fiddle, the other is the bow. By sprinkling water on the "string" strips and running the "bow" across them, a squeaky musical sound was produced. We had a great time with our fiddles. Only a comb with a paper over it and placed on the lips made a more loud musical tone.

Autumn came and the corn turned brown. Frost was in the air . . . it was corn picking time. Dad had a hired man to help him. Each one had a wagon and a team to go out into the fields. A wagon had one side built up higher than the other with boards. These were called bang boards or side boards. As the corn was picked, the ears would be tossed into the wagons. These boards would prevent them from going over the other side. On one hand, Dad wore a husking peg and on the other, a husking hook was fastened to his wrist. The wagons of husked corn were pulled into the barnyard to the corn crib. They were run upon a corn dump where the wagon was tilted, allowing the ears to fall into the conveyor, which in turn, drew them up to the top of the corn crib roof to an opening to one of the two big cribs. Both cribs would be full when the corn was all picked. The corn dump was powered by a horse hitched to the machinery that turned as the animal went around and around in a circle.

Dad gave me a nice ear of corn with all its husks on so I could make a Halloween corn witch. I braided part of the husk on each side of the ear, leaving the back husk on as hair. I took out two kernels for the eyes, one for the nose and several for the mouth at the top of the ear. My mother helped me make a witch's skirt and cape of black material and a hat, too. We used black construction paper. A round piece formed the brim and a rolled up piece formed the tall, tapered hat. We placed the corn witch in a glass and she would stand alone, her skirt falling down around the edge of the glass. I created a corn stalk broom from the top part of a stalk, about five or six inches long. I shredded some husk for the broom and tied it to the stick. After pinning it to the witch's skirt, I had a completed Halloween decoration to place next to the jack-o-lantern.

Several times a season, Dad would find a rare red ear of corn and would give it to me. I always kept those. They were so pretty.

Winter had arrived. The corn had all been picked. It started to snow on the cornfield. I watched the snow and heard it ticking on the brown and bent corn stalks. The wind blew harder and the snow fell faster, almost hiding the cornstalks. Another year had ended. The corn field looked tired . . . winter was rest time. It had yielded well and we had enjoyed the abundance.

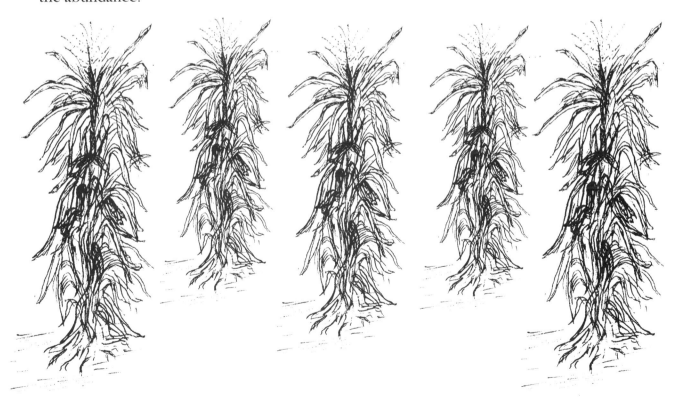

Autumn Time

*Autumn has touched the hill-side
With colors of red and gold;
The valley lay in silvery mist,
As the morning hours unfold.
The fodder shocks stand in the fields,
The husks are brown and sere;
And pumpkins lie upon the ground
When autumn time is here.*

*At noon, the silvery cobwebs
Float on the autumn air;
And flocks of birds wing their way,
To climes more warm and fair.
The scarlet maples lean o'er the stream,
Where water flows deep and clear;
Reflecting beauty in its depths
When autumn time is here.*

*The sun goes down in misty haze
There's wood smoke in the air;
The pines are dark against the sky,
Etched in beauty rare.
The days grow less in sunlit hours,
The longer nights are near;
A farewell to the leaves and flowers
When autumn time is here.*

October Days

When frost is in the air,
And withered husk on the maize:
Woodlands painted everywhere,
To tell you, "It's October Days".

When nuts are ripe and squirrels are out,
And the sun has shortened it's rays:
Leaving in your mind no doubt,
"It's October Days".

Autumn's chill is in the breeze,
And the last of flowers nods and waves:
Bidding farewell to the leaves,
For it's October Days".

When the air is filled with snow,
And no longer the misty haze;
Lingers where the river flows,
Then it's goodbye "October Days".

September Dreams

September's here with golden dreams;
Flowers reflected in the streams,
Mornings come with rosy mist;
Clusters of grapes with dew are kissed.

Apples ripening red and yellow;
Russet pears are getting mellow,
Over all the sky of blue;
With the swallows skimming through.

Loudly now the crickets sing;
In the distance cowbells ring,
And shafts of golden sunlight gleams,
Weaving our September Dreams.

Christmas With Real Candles

Excitement was high on a Christmas Eve many years ago . . . I was sitting in a semi-circle with my brothers and sisters, waiting for our Dad to light the candles on the Christmas Tree. The hanging lamp in its bracket holder by the pantry door with its bright reflector was burning bright, but not enough to dim the candles on the tree. The stockings were hung on a line, all seven of them, with name tags at the top of each. Limply hanging, waiting for Santa, who would be coming through the big front door. It was always left unlocked on Christmas Eve. Coming down the chimney was unthinkable, with our six inch stove pipe. Maybe a fireplace chimney with the fire out, but not our chimney.

Dad lighted a match and we all sat still as he carefully lit the six inch tall assorted color candles that were firmly placed in clip-on holders. The last one was lit and he stepped back and sat in his chair, admiring the flickering effect of the lit tapers. The pungent pine tree with its icicles, red and green roping and adored tinsel garland shone beautifully in the flickering candle light. The homemade star of cardboard with tinsel garland over it was the focal point of the decorations and for a few precious moments, we were transfixed to the beauty.

The stocking line dimly showing up with the limp stockings could be visioned bulging after Santa had come. It was a memory burned into my mind . . . the beauty, the expectancy and the love that encircled the entire family. It continued, even when the last shining candle had been snuffed out.

Winter's Night,
   cold, frozen and Silent.

Forty Years Later . . .

My husband, George, and I enjoyed a lovely ride on a Sunday afternoon. It was a golden Autumn day and a pleasant trip into the misty past for me. We stopped at the old home where I spent my early childhood. The big house was empty and I looked through the dusty windows to see again my childhood home. I turned the knob and the door squeaked open. I stepped across a threshold I had not crossed in forty years . . .

I showed George the living room where I had played and where the Christmas tree stood every year . . . the pantry where I accidentally upset a crock of milk. We stepped into the parlor where the sun had once shown golden through the ecru lace curtains onto the rug. At the north parlor door, we always found snap bugs when it was opened for the summer months. The parlor bedroom had a closet under the stairs. In the upstairs bedrooms, we saw a fantastic view of the farm. There was Hazel and Marie's room with the three-cornered closet. Ray's room was adjacent, and I remembered them playing childhood games. Each had a King Ruler, but the game broke up when Ray, announced he had killed his King. The kitchen, downstairs, had the same sink and cistern pump. I pointed to the east kitchen window where the glass pane had a small break in one corner, as it did then. As a child, I would peek through it and see the twinkling lights of Geary's house, across the snowy pasture. How well I remembered! In the washroom, the basement door was situated in the center of the room. One night, "Old Dan," the hired man fell. We children had accidentally left the door open and down the stairs he went, spraining his neck. "Diamond", a neighbor man, called him "Old Rubberneck" after that. I opened the door and the same darkness met my gaze, as it had done so many years ago. I had wanted an apple from the barrel downstairs, but Marie and Ray were there, making scary noises so I wouldn't go down in the dark. I just stared into the darkness and smelled the odor of the ripening apples.

The north porch was wide as the house. I looked under it, remembering when Hazel had crawled under to the center, and frightened me by growling, "King Kong, King Kong"! Through the dim light, she moved as a dark object. I nearly fainted with fright, and I raced away to the safety of the living room. The living room was large and we had a bracket lamp hung up high by the door with a bright reflector. When company was coming, Dad pulled the Victrola from the parlor to the living room and played Hawaiian records. They put me to sleep as I sat in my chair, waiting for the company to arrive. I missed the refreshments served between 9:30 and 10:30 at night.

Most of the trees were gone . . . even the big box elder tree in the corner of the yard. Dad had nailed some boards to it, making a tree house for Walter and me. One time, we carried a string of wieners up into our tree house. But, before we could eat them, our mother intervened and in no uncertain words, told us the proper time and place to eat wieners. So ended our lunch with only verbal punishment. An old pear tree and a mulberry tree still stood by the garden wall. Also, a scarred old maple and the last of five walnut trees were left in the orchard. The once-shady place was practically barren now. The concrete walk was broken up. I used to watch the leafy, afternoon shadows cross the curve in the walk. That signaled the afternoon. The pond by the water tank was still there with most of the big stones surrounding it. The concrete water tank remained, but the tall windmill, with the metal ladder, where I had climbed half way to the top, was gone.

Most of the old neighbors were gone, too. It had all changed, but still held a thrill of childhood days and the years rolled back. It was a time to remember . . . how it used to be . . . and how soon every thing changes.

Woodland Pause

Pausing in the woodland, in the springtime of the year.
Hear, the myriad voices calling rhythmic and clear.
Birds, to the woodland returning,
From their winter stay—
In the warm and sunny southland,
Dressed in colors gay.
From the silvery waters of the rill, comes the bull-frog's refrain,
Welcoming to the forest, every creeping thing.
Spring beauties dot the hillside,
The air is fresh and clear,
It cheers the heart to rest there—
In the springtime of the year.
Pausing in the woodland on a quiet summer day,
Looking up, through tall trees where the lights and shadows play.
Looking down, upon a meadow,
From this woodland retreat,
While the wafting fragrance rises,
From the clover sweet.
Nesting birds sing blithe-somely as from branch to branch they fly,
And puffy clouds sail lazily through an azure sky,
Lingering for a little while,
our cares to allay,
Thanking God for woodland beauty
On a quiet summer day.
Pausing in the woodland on a bright, autumn day,
Listening to the honking geese on their southward way.
Colored leaves float downward Through the frosty air,
Carpeting the forest floor in autumn beauty rare.
Above, the lines of cobwebs glint in the autumn sky,
The migrating spiders, ride the zephrs high.
Below, the water sparkles as it
winds its way–
Across the wooded acres on the bright autumn day.
Pausing in the woodland on a cold, winter day,
The naked trees, stand stiff and tall,
Against the sky of gray.
The withered leaves lie beneath the snow–
The faded flowers hang low,
Swaying to the eddying breeze, above the drifted snow.
Beneath the snow, the roots hold life
To grow and bloom again—
But, now is the time for the woodland to sleep,
While cold, white beauty reigns.

Love

Love comes slowly to some they say,
Slowly growing it makes its way
to the heart of you or I.
But, I would that it came to me,
On the very fastest wings:
Not a delay must there be:
Or the joy is lost that it brings.

Sunday

The sun arose in skies of gray:
Brightening the hills on its way,
Covering the earth with bright array,
Heralding another new born day.

We Are Blessed

We are blessed when we can find beauty
and contentment in such things as these.
The first patches of green grass on a hillside.
Birds twittering across newly plowed fields,
The droning of bees in blossoming apple trees.
The low serenade of frogs from ponds and marshes.
Gay March winds that blow clothes to fresh dry sweetness.
Soft April rain with a rainbow to remind us again we are blessed.
'Tis Spring with a full new year ahead.

Yesterday

Shall we fret
about the things
We didn't do or say:
Are they really
that important?
Those hopes
of yesterday.
Yesterday has
gone away,
Folded like an
outgrown clock:
In golden silence,
let it lay:
Take from it,
only hope.

Today

Let us not waste
our time away:
Precious now,
is just today,
Do and say the
best you can,
Be friendly with
thy fellow man:
Use today wisely
as you can:
For soon it too,
becomes yesterday.

Tomorrow

Bright and clear
with newborn hope:
We look ahead to
that new day:
When horizons
have a wider scope,
And opportunity
beckons her way:
Taking Hope from
yesterday,
Leaving all
the sorrows:
Using the Best
from today,
Will aid in forming
our tomorrows.

Poems

A sage in reverie sat dreaming,
On a quiet summer's day:
Of a vacant old house still standing:
Near a stream where bright waters play.
Where as a child he lived and loved:
The house and orchard too,
The vines still clinging round the door:
With flowers of misty blue.
Father coming from the field:
The weary horses plod:
Eager for a night of rest ere
again they turn the sod.
Memories of a farmers boy,
Bringing home the cattle:
Happy and free and full of joy,
He's ready for Life's battles.

March Winds

March winds blowing through the night,
Carrying snow in its forward flight,
Scurring across the meadow wide,
Sweeping the fields on either side.
Over the woodland swaying the trees.
Breaking dead branches loosening dry leaves.
Hurrying through forest and waste,
Piling snow high in its haste.
Constant and strong all through the night.
March wind whistles in onward flight,
Until the wintery blasts blow low,
Leaving behind white drifts of snow.
Dark clouds lift, the sky turns blue.
The night is gone and the March winds too.

Silent Fields

The faded flowers of Summer
Have long been lost to view,
The heavy rains of Autumn
Turned brown their brilliant hue.

Across the silent fields
The snow in silence lay,
Touched only by the sunsets glow
At the end of a winters day.

Song Sparrow

The clouds hang low a misty gray,
In the early dawn of a springtime day.
While the song sparrow sings his melody gay
From over the meadow across the way.

There's tinges of green on the banks of the stream
With moss covered stones lying between.
Above sings the song sparrow lilting and gay
From over the meadow across the way.

The squirrel leaps through the leafless trees
Nibbling new buds Spring's delicacy
While the sparrow watches the squirrel at play
From over the meadow across the way.

Wee harbinger of Spring so lithesome and gay
Your song brings gladness to the dark day
Wild-bird! keep singing your roundelay,
From over the meadow across the way.

When you were here

When you were here,
We walked the woodland path:
Just we two,
The little home we'd longed to buy:
Was at last, our dream come true.

You cut the saplings and cleared our wood,
Together we roamed the fields:
The land we farmed was fairly good,
And turned out a bounteous yield.

We gathered nuts from the woods,
For wintery days ahead:
Brought in the pumpkins from the fields,
Filled up the old woodshed.

Life was richer, gayer far,
When I could walk and talk with you.
But now I miss those bygone days,
When you were here with me.
But feel your presence in every place,
Just as it used to be.

Written for my Mother after my Dad had passed on.

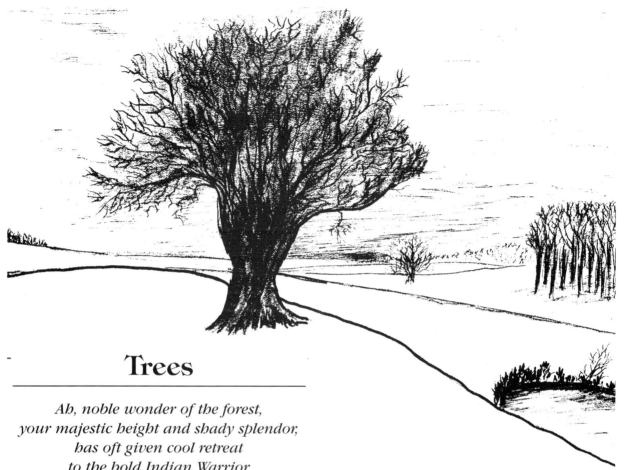

Trees

Ah, noble wonder of the forest,
your majestic height and shady splendor,
has oft given cool retreat
to the bold Indian Warrior
who sought rest from
noon day sun.

Then, as now, trees are
man's greatest living possession.
May we strive to protect them;
for as long as civilization exists,
the need of these stalwart
defenders of man are
indeed essential to our
present and future progress
and national defense
of America.

No problem is too difficult,
that it cannot be solved
by intelligent thinking.
April, 27, 1941